Farmyard Friends
DUCKS

Maddie Gibbs

PowerKiDS
press.

New York

Dedication: *For Ellie Johnson*

Published in 2015 by The Rosen Publishing Group, Inc.
29 East 21st Street, New York, NY 10010

First Edition

Editor: Caitie McAneney
Book Design: Katelyn Heinle

Photo Credits: Cover, p. 1 BGSmith/Shutterstock.com; p. 5 Inozemtsev Konstantin/Shutterstock.com; pp. 6, 24 (webbed feet) MVPhoto/Shutterstock.com; p. 9 Hepburn Photography/Shutterstock.com; p. 10 No:veau/Shutterstock.com; p. 13 Michal Lazor/Shutterstock.com; pp. 14, 24 (ducklings) Africa Studio/Shutterstock.com; p. 17 Dalibor Sevaljevic/Shutterstock.com; p. 18 Stargazer/Shutterstock.com; pp. 21 Andersen Ross/Blend Images/Getty Images; p. 22 herjua/Shutterstock.com; p. 24 (feathers) Elfriedchen/Shutterstock.com; p. 24 (quilt) Kellis/Shutterstock.com.

Library of Congress Cataloging-in-Publication Data

Gibbs, Maddie, author.
 Ducks / Maddie Gibbs.
     pages cm. — (Farmyard friends)
 Includes index.
 ISBN 978-1-4994-0100-4 (pbk.)
 ISBN 978-1-4994-0102-8 (6 pack)
 ISBN 978-1-4994-0098-4 (library binding)
 1. Ducks—Juvenile literature. 2. Domestic animals—Juvenile literature. I. Title.
 SF505.3.G53 2015
 636.5'97—dc23
                                    2014025265

Manufactured in the United States of America

CPSIA Compliance Information: Batch #CW15PK: For Further Information contact Rosen Publishing, New York, New York at 1-800-237-9932

CONTENTS

Ducks are birds. Some ducks live in the wild. Some ducks live on farms.

Ducks have **webbed feet**.
This helps them swim.

There are many different kinds of ducks. Call ducks are the smallest.

Pekin ducks are the most common kind. They first came from China.

Indian runner ducks are tall. They do not walk like other ducks. They run instead.

Male ducks are called drakes. Baby ducks are called **ducklings**.

Mother ducks lay eggs.
Ducklings break out of eggs
after about 28 days.

People raise ducks for their meat, eggs, and **feathers**. Some are raised to be pets.

A duck's inner feathers are called down. People make warm coats and **quilts** with down.

21

It is fun to see ducks on a farm. You might even get to pet them!

WORDS TO KNOW

ducklings

feathers

quilt

webbed feet

INDEX

WEBSITES

Due to the changing nature of Internet links, PowerKids Press has developed an online list of websites related to the subject of this book. This site is updated regularly. Please use this link to access the list: www.powerkidslinks.com/fmyd/duck